Inside the Ants' Nest

by Karen Ang

Consultants:

Brian L. Fisher
Chairman, Department of Entomology, California Academy of Sciences, San Francisco

Kimberly Brenneman, PhD
National Institute for Early Education Research, Rutgers University, New Brunswick, New Jersey

BEARPORT
PUBLISHING

New York, New York

Credits
Cover, © iStockphoto/ThinkStock; 3, © iStockphoto/Thinkstock; 4, © Fir4ik/Shutterstock; 5, © Alan J.S. Weaving/Ardea; 7, © Andrey Pavlov/Shutterstock; 8, © TTPhoto/Shutterstock; 9, © NataliSuns/Shutterstock, © Paul Rommer/Shutterstock, © Triff/Shutterstock, © Andrey Starostin/Shutterstock, and © asharkyu/Shutterstock; 10, © Khemporn Tongphay/Shutterstock; 11, © foto76/Shutterstock; 12, © Roger Eritja/Biosphoto/FLPA; 13, © Minden Pictures/Superstock; 14, 15T, © Eric Isselee/Shutterstock; 15, © Hiroya Minakuchi/Minden Pictures/FLPA; 16, © Viktor Cap/Alamy; 17, © Oxford Scientific/Getty Images; 18, 19, © Dwight Kuhn Photography; 20, © Alex Wild Photography; 21, © Fir0002/Flagstaffotos; 23TL, © Anest/Shutterstock; 23TC, © Mark Moffett/Minden Pictures/FLPA; 23TR, © Andrey Pavlov/Shutterstock; 23BL, © Alex Wild Photography; 23BC, © Oxford Scientific/Getty Images; 23BR, © Dwight Kuhn Photography; 24, © iStockphoto/Thinkstock.

Publisher: Kenn Goin
Senior Editor: Joyce Tavolacci
Creative Director: Spencer Brinker
Design: Emma Randall
Photo Researcher: Ruby Tuesday Books Ltd

Library of Congress Cataloging-in-Publication Data

Ang, Karen.
  Inside the ants' nest / by Karen Ang ; consultant, Brian Fisher.
    p. cm. — (Snug as a bug: where bugs live)
  Includes bibliographical references and index.
  ISBN-13: 978-1-61772-902-7 (library binding) — ISBN-10: 1-61772-902-7 (library binding)
  1. Ant communities—Juvenile literature. 2. Ants—Juvenile literature. 3. Insect societies—
Juvenile literature. I. Fisher, Brian L., 1964– II. Title.
  QL568.F7A54 2014
  595.79'61782—dc23
                                          2013011030

Copyright © 2014 Bearport Publishing Company, Inc. All rights reserved. No part of this publication may be reproduced in whole or in part, stored in any retrieval system, or transmitted in any form or by any means, electronic, mechanical, photocopying, recording, or otherwise, without written permission from the publisher.

For more information, write to Bearport Publishing Company, Inc., 45 West 21st Street, Suite 3B, New York, New York 10010. Printed in the United States of America.

10 9 8 7 6 5 4 3 2 1

Contents

Welcome to the Nest

ant

nest hole

It's early morning, and the sun is peeking through some trees in a forest.

A tiny **insect** marches out of a hole in the ground.

It's followed by hundreds of others that look just like it.

The little insects are ants leaving their underground nest to search for food.

ants leaving their nest

An ants' nest is a home where the insects rest, eat, and raise their young.

What Is an Ant?

Where ants live

Ants live in every part of the world except Antarctica, Iceland, and Greenland.

Like all insects, ants have three main body parts, six legs, and two **antennae**.

There are more than 14,000 different kinds of ants.

The largest ants are more than one inch (2.5 cm) long.

The smallest ones are only about the size of a comma.

Ants can be black, brown, red, or even bright orange.

three main body parts

legs

antennae

What parts of an ant's body do you think are used to dig a nest?

7

Underground Nests

anthill

When building their nests, some ants carry the dirt that is left over from digging and pile it on top of their underground homes. These large mounds are called anthills.

Ants live with thousands of other ants in homes called nests.

Many kinds of ants build their nests underground.

To make a nest, ants use their mouths and legs to dig tunnels in the dirt.

At the end of the tunnels, they create special rooms called chambers.

Within the chambers, ants lay eggs, raise babies, store food, and rest.

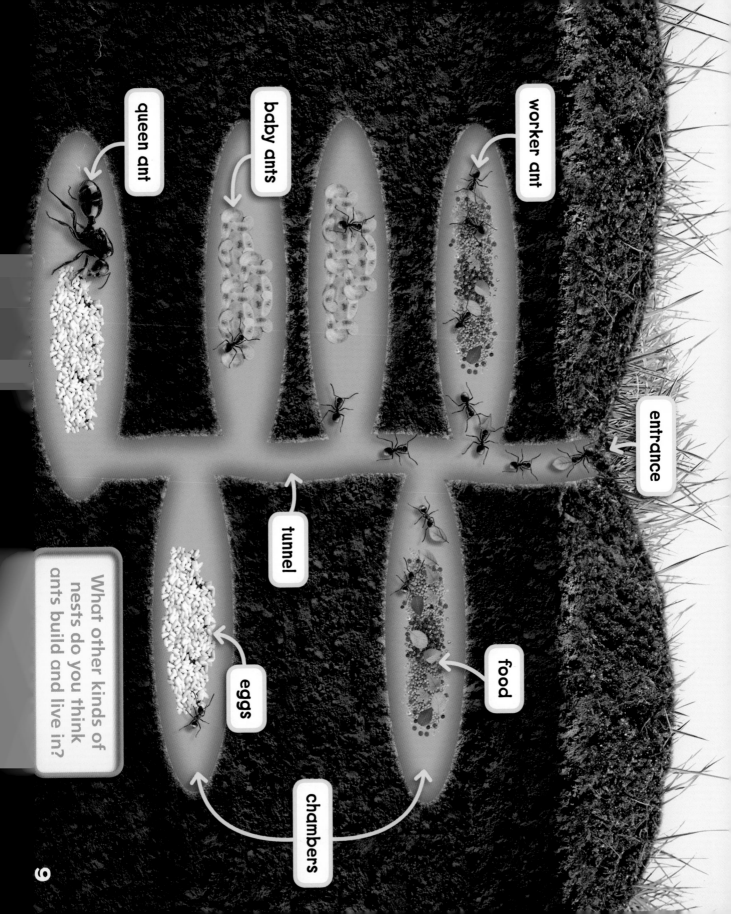

queen ant

baby ants

worker ant

entrance

tunnel

food

eggs

chambers

What other kinds of
nests do you think
ants build and live in?

9

In the Trees

Not all ants build underground homes.

Some ants make their nests high above the ground in trees.

They work as a team to pull tree leaves together to make tentlike nests.

To hold the leaves in place, the ants use sticky silk made by their young.

The ants pull the silk across the leaf edges to stick the leaves together.

ants pulling leaves together

weaver ant nest

silk

Ants that weave together leaves to build nests are sometimes called weaver ants.

What types of jobs do you think ants do in the nest?

An Ant Colony

male ant

Ants live together in family groups called colonies.

There are three kinds of ants in a colony: the queen, female workers, and males.

The queen lays eggs that grow into baby ants.

Worker ants build the nest.

They also take care of the baby ants, find food, and protect the colony.

The male ants' only job is to mate with other queen ants.

Hungry Ants

worker ant collecting fruit

To feed a colony, worker ants must collect a lot of food.

They search for plants, seeds, fruit, and insects to bring back to the nest.

Some kinds of ants grow their own food inside their nests!

Leaf-cutter ants grow **fungus** in special chambers.

As the fungus grows, worker ants collect it and feed it to baby ants.

leaf-cutter ants

Leaf-cutter ants use their strong mouthparts to cut leaves and carry them back to the nest. They then crush the leaves and place them on the fungus to help it grow.

Protecting the Nest

giant anteater

Nests aren't always safe places for ants.

Many kinds of animals attack ants' homes to eat the insects inside.

For example, anteaters push their long, sticky tongues into nests to catch ants.

Aardvarks and brown bears break open nests to get to the ants inside.

To protect the colony, large workers called soldier ants bite and sting these enemies.

soldier ant

Ants can let
each other know
that danger is near
by releasing smelly
chemicals called
pheromones from
their bodies.

How do you
think ants begin
their lives?

From Egg to Adult

eggs

Ants begin their lives as tiny, round eggs.

The queen lays the eggs inside special chambers in the nest.

After a few days, wormlike larvae hatch from the eggs.

Workers care for and feed the larvae, which then change into **pupae**.

The pupae develop eyes, legs, and antennae as they grow into adults.

How do you think new ant colonies form?

larvae

pupae

It can take two months or longer for larvae to become adult ants.

A New Nest

queen

male ant

Most pupae grow up and become worker ants.

However, some pupae will become queens.

The new queens will fly away to mate with males and start building new nests.

In a short time, they will be home to thousands of ants!

Queen ants can live for 20 to 40 years. Most worker ants, however, live for a year or two.

queen ant digging a new nest

Science Lab

Draw a Diagram

Imagine you are a scientist studying a colony of ants in their underground nest. Draw a diagram on a piece of paper that shows how ants live.

Read the questions below and think about the answers. You can include this information in your diagram.

What are the different parts of an ants' nest?

What do the different ants do inside the nest?

Why is the nest a good place for ants to live?

After you finish the diagram, present it to your friends and family.

How to draw a nest

1. Use a pencil to draw a line across the top of the paper.

2. Below the line, shade the rest of the page with your pencil.

3. Then use an eraser to create tunnels and chambers in the shaded area.

4. Draw some worker ants, food, a queen, eggs, larvae, and pupae in the different chambers.

5. Include labels that tell what the main parts of the nest are. Also, include labels that tell some things that ants do inside and outside their nest.

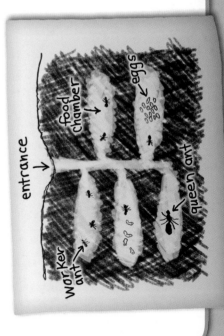

Science Words

antennae (an-TEN-ee)
the two body parts on
an insect's head used for
feeling and smelling

mate (MAYT) to come
together to have young

fungus (FUHN-guhss)
a plantlike organism that
can't make its own food,
such as a mushroom

pheromones (FAIR-uh-mohns)
chemicals made by an animal
to send a message to another
animal

insect (IN-sekt) a small animal
that has six legs, three main
body parts, two antennae,
and a hard covering called
an exoskeleton

pupae (PYOO-pee) young
insects at the stage of
development between
larvae and adults

23

Index

Read More

Aronin, Miriam. *The Ant's Nest: A Huge, Underground City (Spectacular Animal Towns).* New York: Bearport (2010).

Lock, Deborah. *Ant Antics.* New York: DK (2012).

Stewart, Melissa. *Ants.* Washington, DC: National Geographic (2010).

Learn More Online

To learn more about ants and their nests, visit www.bearportpublishing.com/SnugasaBug

About the Author

Karen Ang has worked on many books about science, nature, and animals. She lives in Connecticut, where she watches ants build their nests in the fields near her home.